Decorative
Papercutting

Lady Boutique Series No. 3346 Otona Kawaii Kirigami Zuanshuu
Copyright © 2011 Boutique-Sha, Inc.

Originally published in Japanese language by Boutique-Sha, Tokyo, Japan
English language rights, translation & production by World Book Media, LLC
Email: info@worldbookmedia.com

Japanese Language Edition Staff:
Editor: Kanako Yaguchi and Kumiko Kosakai
Photography: Ritsuko Fujita
Book Design: Makiko Umemiya
Illustrations: Tamaki Ozaki

English Translation: Yoh Sasaki
English Language Editor: Lindsay Fair

Published in the United States of America by STACKPOLE BOOKS
5067 Ritter Road, Mechanicsburg, PA 17055
www.stackpolebooks.com

ISBN 978-0-8117-1232-3

Printed in China

10 9 8 7 6 5 4 3 2 1
Cataloging-in-Publication data is on file with the Library of Congress.

Decorative
Papercutting

Instructions and Patterns for
150 Intricate Cutouts

STACKPOLE
BOOKS

Contents

Part 1: Project Gallery

Part 2: Project Instructions

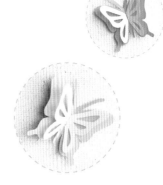

Introduction

Papercutting is a fun and artful hobby that is accessible to everyone. Little is needed to get started, and most households will already have the basics on hand: paper and scissors. It is amazing what can be created with just a few folds, snips, and the careful unfolding of paper.

In this book, I'll introduce a clear set of folding methods and full-size templates for all of the motifs featured in this book.

Take a few simple motifs and join them with string to create a decorative mobile. Or take a completed design and glue to cardstock to embellish a handmade greeting card or gift box.

Experiment with a common paper item, like an envelope, to create a unique circular project, such as a little wreath or crown, that doesn't even require glue!

While some designs are easy and can be executed without too much effort, other designs are more intricate and will require a bit more focus and time. With the enclosed directions and templates, all of the designs and projects are achievable—even for the beginner!

I hope you enjoy making and using these beautiful papercutting designs!

—Akiko Murooka

Part 1
Project Gallery

Spring Has Sprung

These bright and cheerful designs celebrate the sweetness of spring. Throw a party to welcome the arrival of the season and use these delightful designs to adorn the walls and windows.

1 *Bluebirds/65*
2 *Butterfly Trio/65*
3 *Green Leaves/65*
4 *Lovely Ladybugs/65*
5 *Songbirds/66*
6 *Hungry Hedgehogs/66*

Down on the Farm

Create a playful pastoral view for a kid's room with these friendly farm animals. Don't forget the green grass for grazing!

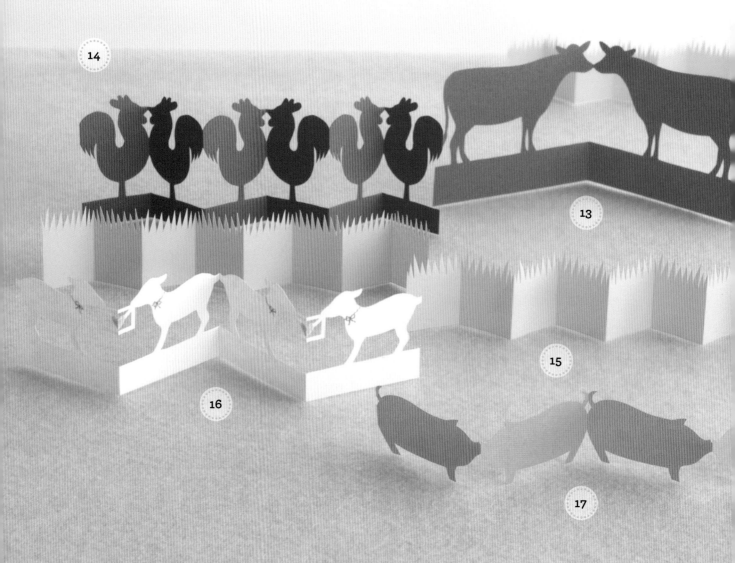

The Paper Ocean

Make a splash with these nautical themed papercutting designs. All the motifs in this collection use the simple accordion fold method, so it will be nothing but smooth sailing.

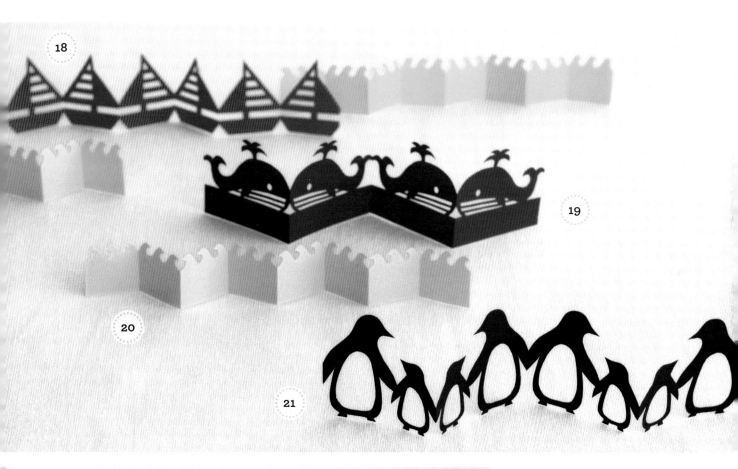

Paper Play Date

Create a fantasy play date with paper! Use these happy-go-lucky designs to decorate a gift for the special girl in your life.

24

25

26

27

28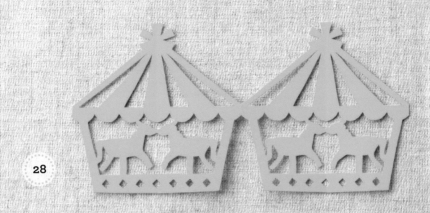

29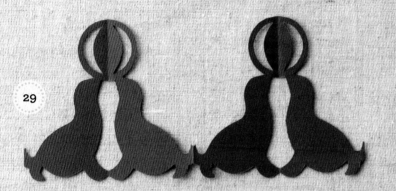

30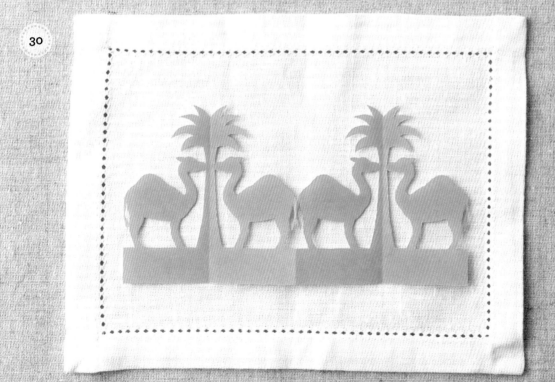

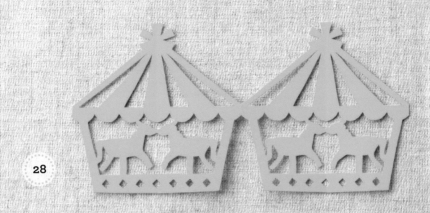

An Elegant Edge

Use these neat and sweet edge motifs just about anywhere! Try them on handmade cards, personalized place settings, or as windowsill decorations.

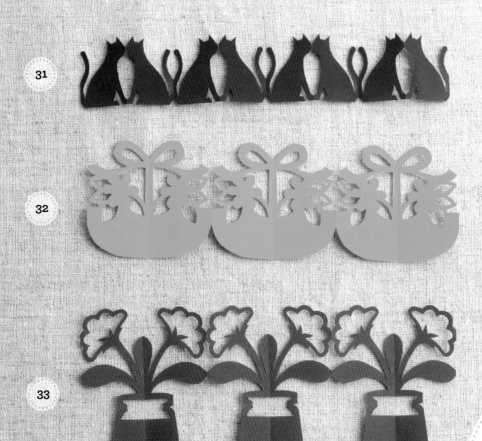

31

32

33

34

3-D Papercutting Decor

Give your papercutting some dimension and explore another side of this art form. Make these 3-D decorative paper projects by adding a little glue to the mix. They will look great from every angle!

Scroll Doily shown on page 33

Curious Creatures

With their bright colors and bold designs, these cute critters make a statement. Frame one of these fun designs for a whimsical piece of artwork that showcases your papercutting skills.

39 *Frolicking Frogs/78*
40 *Party Parrots/78*

41 *Bouncing Bunnies*/79
42 *Nutty Squirrels*/79

Snowflake Soiree

One of the most classic papercutting motifs, these pretty paper snow-flakes are great as window decorations and tree ornaments, but the sky is the limit when it comes to using these fancy flurries!

43 *Eight Point Flake/80*
44 *Quilted Flake/80*
45 *Lace Flake/80*
46 *Carnival Flake/80*

47 *Star Flake*/81
48 *Poinsettia Flake*/81
49 *Firework Flake*/81
50 *Diamond Flake*/82

Signs of Spring

No green thumb? Cultivate a paper garden for every season. Welcome spring with these early bloomers. Use bright hues to add cheer to any room.

51

52

53

54

51 *Gerbera Daisy*/82
52 *Cherry Blossom*/82
53 *Cherry Blossom Petals*/82
54 *Dandelions*/83

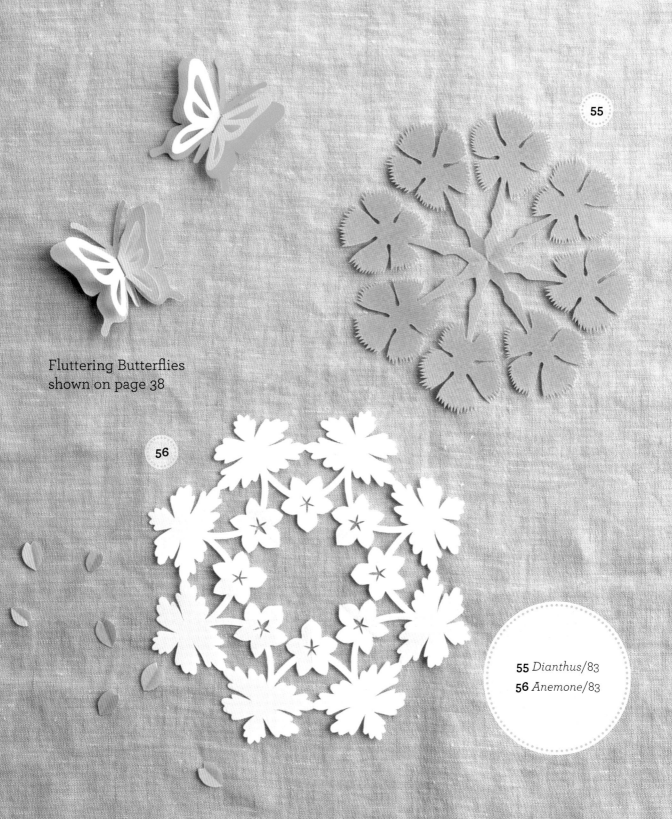

55

Fluttering Butterflies
shown on page 38

56

55 *Dianthus*/83
56 *Anemone*/83

Summer Stunners

These summer flowers feature a vibrant array of colors. Use deep purples and blues for morning glories and bright yellows for sunflowers.

57 *Lily of the Valley*/85
58 *Sunflower*/84
59 *Roses*/85

60 *Daylily*/83
61 *Large Hydrangea*/84
62 *Small Hydrangea*/84
63 *Morning Glory*/85

Autumn Accents

Choose rich, earthy colors for these fall favorites. Chrysanthemums dazzle in shades of yellow, while ginkgo and maple leaves shine in gold.

64 *Ginkgo and Maple/84*
65 *Small Dragonfly/86*
66 *Large Dragonfly/86*
67 *Red Spider Lily/86*

70

71

68

69

Winter Winners

Celebrate the season with these robust winter blooms. Opt for reds, pinks, and whites to coordinate with your other holiday decorations.

72 *Camellia*/87
73 *Cyclamen*/88
74 *Japanese Plum*/88

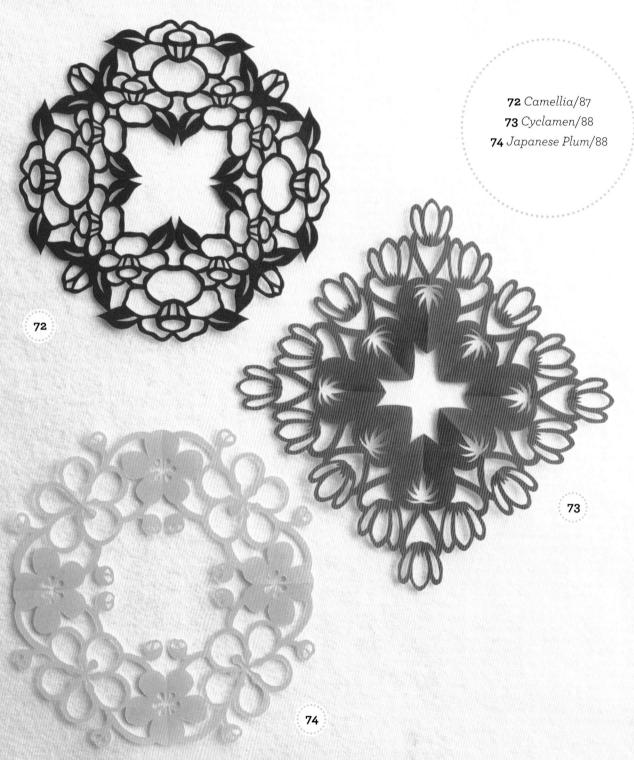

72

73

74

75 *Large Snowflake*/88
76 *Small Snowflake*/88
77 *Small Star Snowflake*/89
78 *Christmas Rose*/89
79 *Large Star Snowflake*/89
80 *Sacred Bamboo*/89

Always in Bloom

These classic designs are perfect for any occasion. Perennial favorites include daisies, daffodils, and carnations.

81 *Clovers/90*
82 *Daisies/90*
83 *Zinnia/90*

84 *Daffodil*/91
85 *Large Roses*/91
86 *Carnation*/91

Leaf Motifs

These lovely leaves can be used to complement floral designs, although their intricate patterns make them surefire standouts.

87

88

89

90

91

92

See page 62 for step-by-step
instructions for 92 Traditional
Leaves

93 *Field of Leaves*/93
94 *Fern*/93

Lovely Lace

Add a touch of class with these beautiful lace designs. The doilies are an easy way to add elegance to table settings, while the trim motifs are perfect for embellishing cards and scrapbooks.

98

99

100

101

102 *Ribbon Lace*/95
103 *Flower Lace*/95
104 *Stitched Lace*/95

102
103
104

105 *Bow Lace*/95
106 *Shamrock Lace*/96
107 *Heart Lace*/96

105
106
107

Circular Centerpieces

Cut from envelopes, these ingenious circular designs make wonderfully unique centerpieces. The crowns lend a regal atmosphere to any kid's party, while the flowers or birds are perfect for everyday use.

108 *King's Crown*/96
109 *Queen's Crown*/96
110 *Flower Wreath*/97
111 *Lovebirds*/97
112 *Village*/97
113 *Matrioshkas*/97

Terrific Traditions

Celebrate Japanese culture with the art of papercutting! Adorned with traditional Japanese symbols, such as plum blossoms and bamboo leaves, these graceful mobiles and money holders are perfect for welcoming in the new year.

Love is in the Air

Spread the love with these symbols of sweetness. Choose red or pink paper for traditional Valentine's Day cards and decorations, or opt for white or pastel hues to celebrate a wedding or birthday.

118 *Heartstrings*/101
119-121 *Fluttering Butterflies*/102
122 *Butterfly Swarm*/103

Decorate your walls with these symbols of love.

123 *Bow Banner*/101
124 *Cheers Chain*/101
125 *Four of Hearts*/101
126-128 *Sweet Straws*/103
129-130 *Butterfly Bags*/102

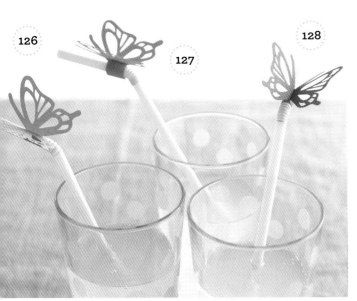

For a special touch, add butterflies to the straws and watch them take flight!

Create custom gift wrap or make party favor bags that will be adored.

This sweet cupcake design is perfect for a birthday card.

Create custom place settings by adding these decorative hearts to plain cups. If you assign each guest a different color, these hearts will serve as drink markers—beautiful and functional all in one.

Haunted Halloween

Haunt your own house with these spooky Halloween-themed designs. Bats, ghosts, and jack-o'-lanterns conspire to create decorations that are simply out of this world.

These spooky sights make perfect wall decorations for a Halloween party.

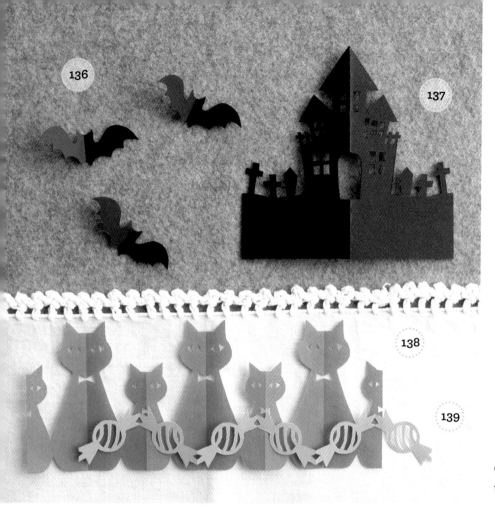

Combine motifs to create a unique, multi-colored design.

This classic Halloween motif makes a perfect design for cards, party invitations, and place cards.

Use battery-operated candles to give this haunted house an eerie glow.

Winter Wonderland

Make the holidays more festive than ever with these symbols of the season. Use these merry motifs to trim your tree, adorn your home, and embellish your cards and wrapping.

142
143
144
145

142 *Deck the Halls*/108
143 *Santa's Boots*/108
144 *Smitten Mittens*/108
145 *Plentiful Presents*/108

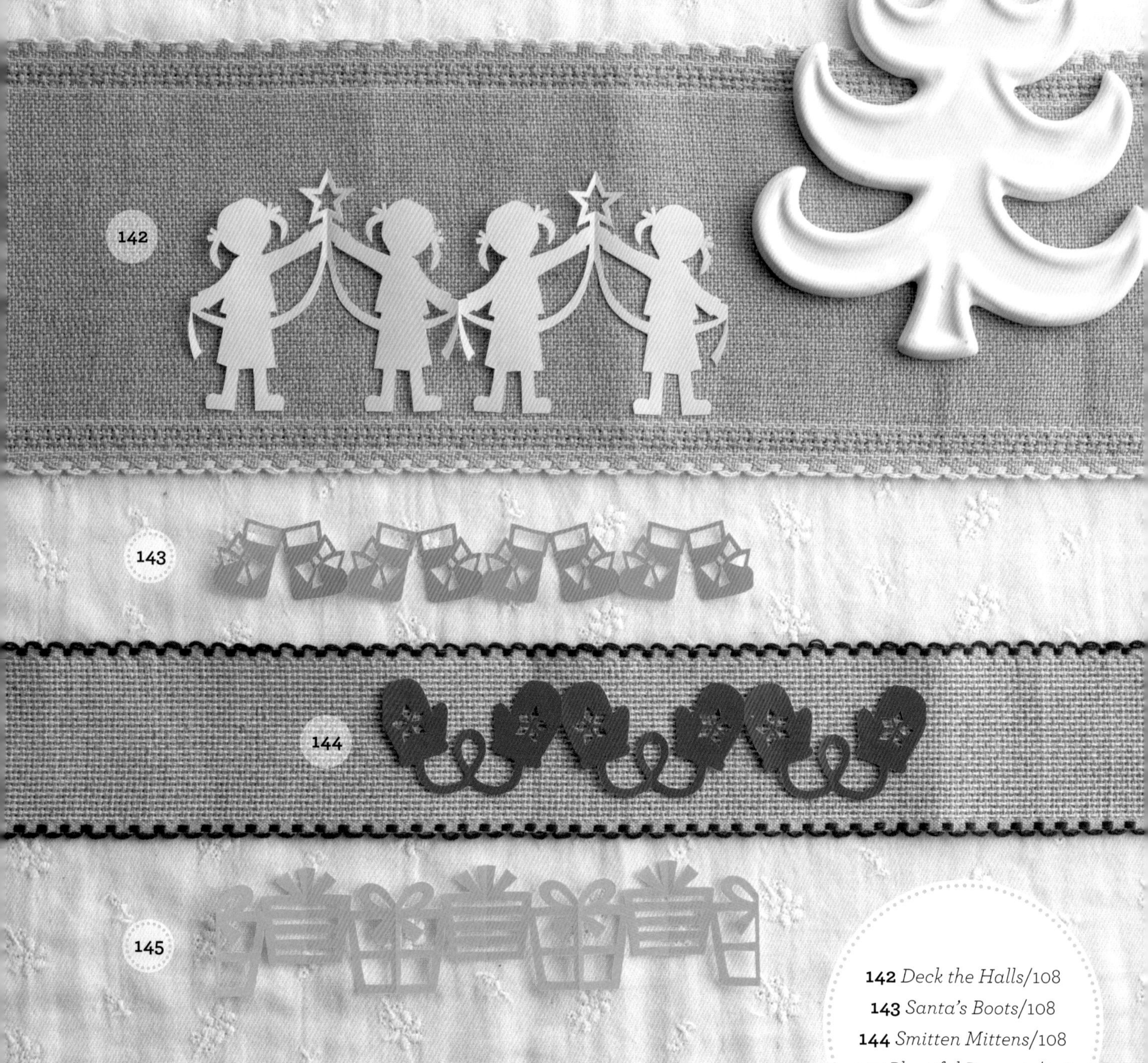

Send some holiday
cheer with this fun
and festive card.

Use this festive outdoor scene to decorate a tabletop.

This wreath design features traditional holiday flowers and will last all season!

149

This beautiful mobile makes an elegant winter decoration. Just like the real thing, each snowflake is unique.

150

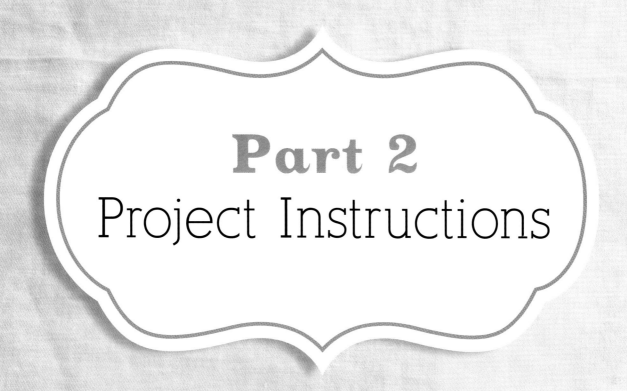

Part 2
Project Instructions

Tools & Materials

The projects in this book don't require specialized tools or hard-to-find materials. You'll just need a few basic items to get started.

Basic Tools

Scissors: Use small, sharp scissors to cut the large outer part of the design. You may prefer to use two pairs of scissors, one larger and one smaller, for greater accuracy.

Cartridge-Style Craft Knife: Use this style craft knife for cutting the smaller, more complicated parts of the pattern, which can be difficult to cut with scissors. A cartridge-style craft knife is suitable for all of the designs in this book.

Pen-Style Craft Knife: Use this style craft knife for even more precision. Both 30° and 45° angled blades are available; however, the standard 30° angle blade is suitable for even the smallest, most complicated designs in this book.

Other Tools

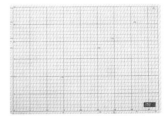

Pencil: Use a sharp pencil to trace the patterns.

Ruler: Use a ruler when tracing patterns with straight lines. A transparent ruler is ideal.

Cutting Mat: Use a cutting mat to protect your work surface when working with a craft knife.

Stapler: Use a stapler to attach a photocopied or traced pattern to the paper before cutting.

Tracing Paper: Use transparent paper to copy the patterns by hand.

Glue Stick: Use a glue stick when constructing projects. Glue sticks provide a neater finish than liquid glue.

Additional Useful Tools

Hollow Punch: Use a hollow punch to make circular holes. A craft knife is suitable for cutting circular holes for the designs in this book; however, you may prefer a hollow punch if you have difficulty cutting smooth curves.

To use a hollow punch, position the paper on top of a scrap of wood. Align the hollow punch and apply pressure while turning.

Paper

6" (15 cm) square sheets

3" (7.5 cm) square sheets

Origami Paper: Use 6" (15 cm) square sheets of origami paper for the majority of designs in this book. Use 3" (7.5 cm) square sheets of origami paper for the smaller designs. Origami paper is ideal for these projects because it is thin, making it easy to cut even when folded several times. Origami paper is available in multi-colored packs at craft supply stores.

Construction Paper: Use this heavier weight paper for making projects such as mobiles and cards. When choosing designs, keep in mind that this paper will be harder to cut out the more it is folded.

Copy Paper: Use 8½" x 11" (21.5 x 28 cm) paper for larger designs. Copy paper is available in many colors at office supply stores.

3½" x 9" (9 x 22.5 cm)

3½" x 8" (9 x 20.5 cm)

Envelopes: Use long, thin envelopes to make circular designs. The designs in this book use 3½" x 8" (9 x 20.5 cm) and 3½" x 9" (9 x 22.5 cm) envelopes, which are available at stationery stores.

Folding Techniques

There are two types of folds used in this book: geometric folds and accordion folds. All of the folds can be made freehand, but we've included a few easy-to-use templates for added precision.

Folding Terms & Symbols

All of the folding techniques in this book use two terms: the valley fold and the mountain fold.

Valley Fold

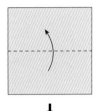

With the right side facing up, fold the paper up so the crease points down. The symbol for a valley fold is a dashed line.

Mountain Fold

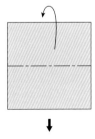

With the right side facing up, fold the paper down so the crease points up. The symbol for a mountain fold is a dashed and dotted line.

Geometric Folds

Single Geometric Fold (creates 2 images)

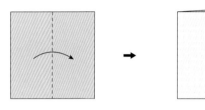

1. With the right side facing up, fold the paper in half vertically to form a rectangle.

2. The single geometric fold is complete.

Double Geometric Fold (creates 4 images)

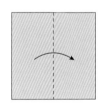 

1. With the right side facing up, fold the paper in half vertically to form a rectangle.

2. With the wrong side facing up, fold the rectangle in half horizontally.

3. The double geometric fold is complete.

Triple Geometric Fold (creates 6 images)

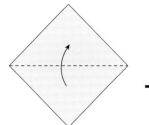 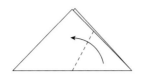

1. With the right side facing up, fold the paper in half to form a triangle.

2. Fold the right corner of the triangle up at a 60° angle using the Triple Geometric Fold template on page 52.

3. Flip the paper over and fold the other corner of the triangle up at a 60° angle to meet the crease made in Step #2.

4. The triple geometric fold is complete.

Quadruple Geometric Fold (creates 8 images)

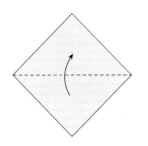 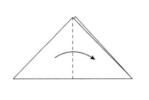

1. With the right side facing up, fold the paper in half to form a triangle.

2. Fold the triangle in half again.

3. Fold the top layer of the right corner up to meet the crease made in Step #2. Flip the paper over and fold the other layer in the same manner.

4. The quadruple geometric fold is complete.

Triple Geometric Fold Template

Use this template for both 3" (7.5 cm) and 6" (15 cm) square sheets of origami paper.

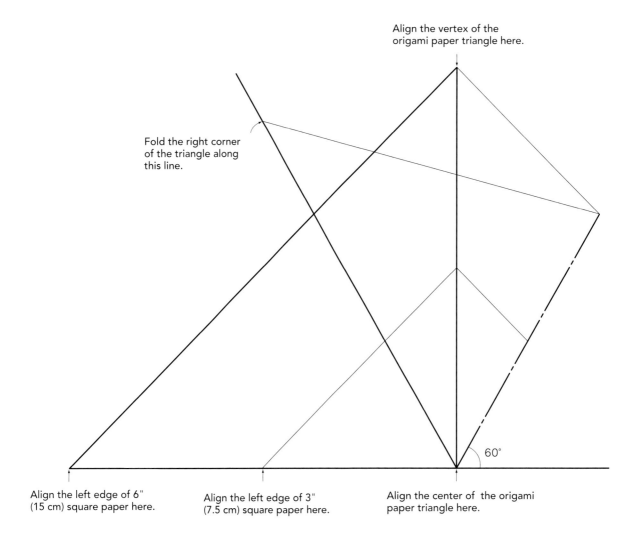

Align the vertex of the origami paper triangle here.

Fold the right corner of the triangle along this line.

60°

Align the left edge of 6" (15 cm) square paper here.

Align the left edge of 3" (7.5 cm) square paper here.

Align the center of the origami paper triangle here.

Accordion Folds

Double Accordion Fold (creates 4 images)

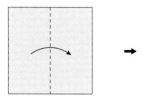 → → 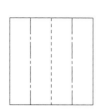 →

1. With the right side facing up, fold the paper in half vertically to form a rectangle.

2. Fold the rectangle in half again.

3. Unfold the paper. You should see 3 creases.

4. With the wrong side facing up, refold the paper along the creases, alternating between mountain and valley folds.

Triple Accordion Fold (creates 6 images)

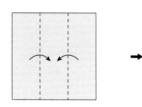 → 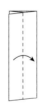 → 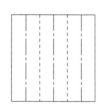 →

1. With the right side facing up, fold the paper into thirds vertically using the Triple Accordion Fold template on page 54.

2. Fold the rectangle in half again.

3. Unfold the paper. You should see 5 creases.

4. With the wrong side facing up, refold the paper along the creases alternating between mountain and valley folds.

Quadruple Accordion Fold (creates 8 images)

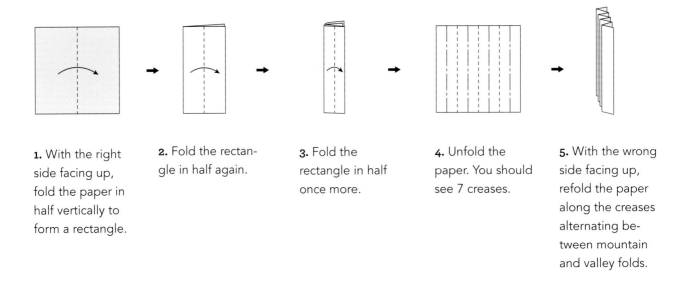

1. With the right side facing up, fold the paper in half vertically to form a rectangle.

2. Fold the rectangle in half again.

3. Fold the rectangle in half once more.

4. Unfold the paper. You should see 7 creases.

5. With the wrong side facing up, refold the paper along the creases alternating between mountain and valley folds.

Triple Accordion Fold Template

Use this template for 6" (15 cm) square sheets of origami paper.

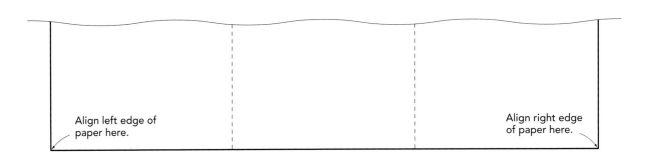

Align left edge of paper here.

Align right edge of paper here.

Envelope Folds

How to Prepare the Envelope Before Folding

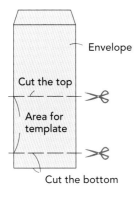

Trim both the top and bottom of the envelope to create a section large enough for the template. There will be two layers of paper since you are using an envelope.

Single Geometric Envelope Fold
(creates 2 images)

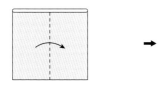

1. Fold the envelope in half vertically to form a rectangle.

2. The single geometric envelope fold is complete.

Triple Accordion Envelope Fold
(creates 3 images)

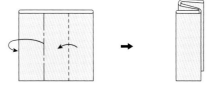

1. Fold the envelope into thirds vertically with one valley fold and one mountain fold using the Triple Accordion Envelope Fold template on page 56.

2. The triple accordion envelope fold is complete.

Triple Accordion Envelope Fold Template

Use this template for 3½" (9 cm) wide envelopes.

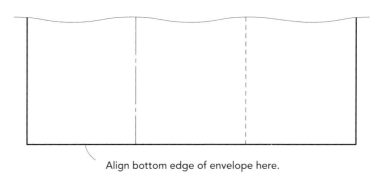

Align bottom edge of envelope here.

Double Accordion Envelope Fold (creates 4 images)

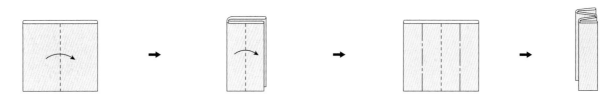

1. Fold the envelope in half vertically to form a rectangle.

2. Fold the rectangle in half again.

3. Unfold the envelope. You should see 3 creases.

4. Refold the envelope along the creases, alternating between mountain and valley folds.

Papercutting Tips

Folding

Folding the paper is easy, just make sure your folds are positioned correctly before you begin cutting. Position the paper with the mountain folds on the left, not the right.

Do

Do position the paper with the mountain folds on the left for a correct and complete design.

Don't

Don't position the mountain folds on the right because this will cause the design to be broken up incorrectly.

Copying

Before you begin cutting, double check that you have copied the design correctly and neatly. This will prevent mistakes.

Positioning the Template

Triple Geometric Fold

Make sure the pattern fits on the paper, or some parts of the design may not come out correctly. This is especially important when using the Triple Geometric Fold because some parts of the paper are not overlapped with this fold. For this fold, make sure the template fits within the shaded area of the paper, as shown in the diagram.

Aligning the Vertex

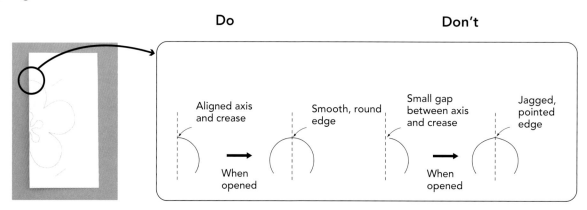

Keep the axis of the template aligned with the crease, not unaligned.

Do align the axis of the template with the crease for smooth, round edges.

Don't leave a space between the template and the crease because this will create jagged, pointed edges.

Cutting

Here are some basics to help with the cutting process. Follow these simple tips for neat, professional-looking designs.

Scissors

Turn the paper, not the scissors.

Do hold the scissors straight and guide the paper into the blades.

Don't turn the scissors to follow the template outline because this will produce inaccurate results.

Use the fulcrum of the scissors, not the tip.

Do use the fulcrum, or part of the scissors where the blades cross, for better maneuverability and precision.

Don't use the tips of the scissors because they cause jagged edges.

Craft Knife

Hold the craft knife straight, not slanted.

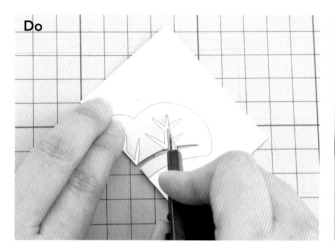

Do

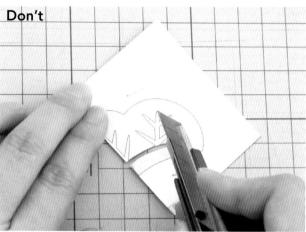

Don't

Do hold the craft knife straight so pressure is applied to the blade evenly.

Don't hold the craft knife angled towards your dominant hand because the blade may snap.

Cutting Curves and Angles

When working on a curved or angled part of the template, it is easier and more accurate to make two separate cuts rather than cutting continuously.

Scissors

1. Make one cut into the vertex of the angle.
2. Remove the scissors and change the angle, then make the other cut into the vertex.

Craft Knife

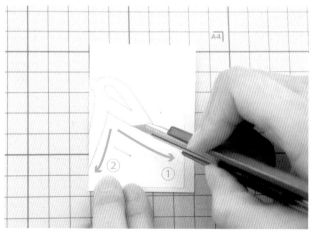

1. Start at the vertex of the angle and cut along one side.
2. Starting at the vertex of the angle again, make a cut along the other side of the angle.

Unfolding

Although you will be excited to unfold your design and reveal the finished project, exercise care and caution to prevent ripping the paper.

1. Smooth out the creases as you unfold the paper.

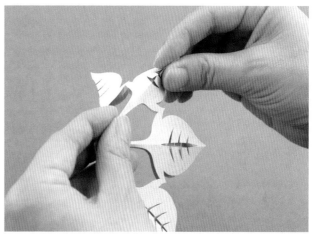

2. Fold the creases in the opposite direction to help flatten the paper.

3. The layers of the paper may stick to each other, so be gentle.

4. Use a rounded object, such as a pen cap, to smooth out the design once it has been unfolded.

Step-by-Step Instructions

93 Traditional Leaves *(Shown on page 31)*

Materials:

One 6" (15 cm) square sheet of origami paper in green

Folding Technique:

Quadruple geometric fold

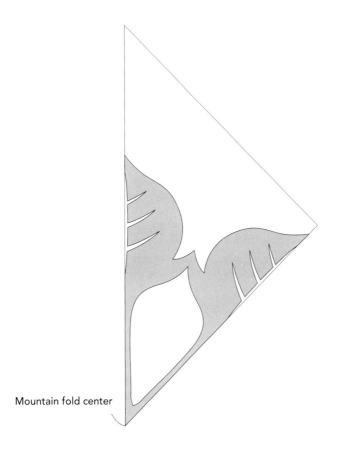

Mountain fold center

Full-Size Template Key

☐ = Area to cut out

▨ = Template

Use the shading system shown above for all of the templates in this book.

1. Fold

1. With the right side facing up, fold the paper in half to form a triangle.

2. Fold the triangle in half again.

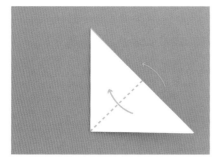

3. Fold the top layer of the right corner up to meet the crease made in Step #2. Flip the paper over and fold the other layer in the same manner.

4. The quadruple geometric fold is complete (refer to page 51 for detailed folding instructions).

2. Copy

Option #1:

Photocopy the template.

1. Photocopy the template and staple it on top of the folded paper. Position the staples on the white part of the template as this part will be cut out (refer to page 58 for detailed copying instructions).

Option #2:

Trace the template.

2. Layer tracing paper on top of the template you wish to transfer and trace the template outline. Staple the template on top of the folded paper, positioning the staples on the white part of the pattern as in Option #1.

3. Cut

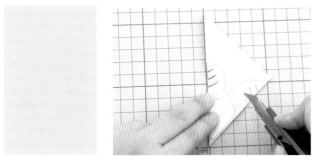

1. Lay the paper on a flat surface and hold it steady with your free hand to prevent it from moving while you cut. Use a craft knife to cut the smaller, more complicated parts first. When cutting, always start from the center of the template and work outwards.

2. The inner cuts are complete.

3. Hold the paper in your hand and make the outer cuts using scissors.

4. The cutting is complete (refer to page 59 for detailed cutting instructions).

4. Unfold

Finished Project

1. The layers of paper may stick together, so unfold the paper gently and smooth it out a little at a time to prevent tearing (refer to page 61 for detailed unfolding instructions).

1 Bluebirds *(Shown on page 8)*

Materials: One 6" (15 cm) square sheet of origami paper in light blue

Folding Technique: Double accordion fold

Mountain fold

2 Butterfly Trio *(Shown on page 8)*

Materials: One 6" (15 cm) square sheet of origami paper in teal

Folding Technique: Triple accordion fold

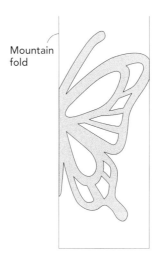

Mountain fold

3 Green Leaves *(Shown on page 8)*

Materials: One 3" (7.5 cm) square sheet of origami paper in green or light green

Folding Technique: Single geometric fold

Mountain fold

4 Lovely Ladybugs *(Shown on page 8)*

Materials: One 3" (7.5 cm) square sheet of origami paper in red or orange

Folding Technique: Single geometric fold

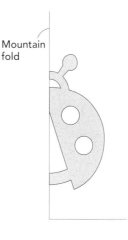

Mountain fold

5 Songbirds *(Shown on page 8)*

Materials: One 6" (15 cm) square sheet of origami paper in brown

Folding Technique: Triple accordion fold

Mountain fold

6 Hungry Hedgehogs
(Shown on page 8)

Materials: One 6" (15 cm) square sheet of origami paper in golden yellow

Folding Technique: Double accordion fold

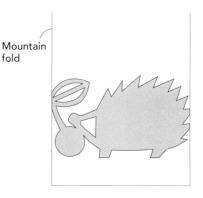

Mountain fold

7 Awesome Acorns *(Shown on page 9)*

Materials: One 6" (15 cm) square sheet of origami paper in brown

Folding Technique: Quadruple accordion fold

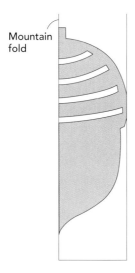

Mountain fold

8 Groovy Grapes *(Shown on page 9)*

Materials: One 6" (15 cm) square sheet of origami paper in purple

Folding Technique: Quadruple accordion fold

Mountain fold

9 Cool Carrots *(Shown on page 9)*

Materials: One 6" (15 cm) square sheet of origami paper in orange

Folding Technique: Quadruple accordion fold

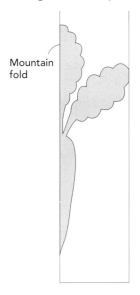

Mountain fold

10 Rad Radishes *(Shown on page 9)*

Materials: One 6" (15 cm) square sheet of origami paper in red

Folding Technique: Quadruple accordion fold

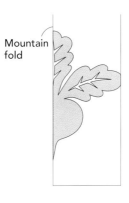

Mountain fold

11 Chatty Rabbits *(Shown on page 9)*

Materials: One 6" (15 cm) square sheet of origami paper in white

Folding Technique: Double accordion fold

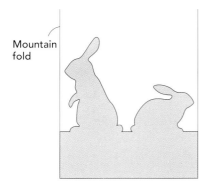

Mountain fold

12 Hungry Squirrels *(Shown on page 9)*

Materials: One 6" (15 cm) square sheet of origami paper in brown

Folding Technique: Quadruple accordion fold

Mountain fold

13 Kissing Cows *(Shown on page 10)*

Materials: One 6" (15 cm) square sheet of origami paper in brown

Folding Technique: Single geometric fold

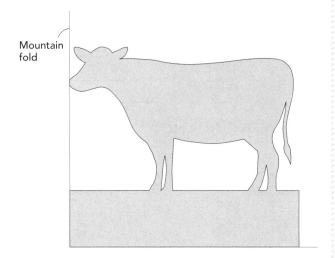

Mountain fold

14 Red Roosters *(Shown on page 10)*

Materials: One 6" (15 cm) square sheet of origami paper in red

Folding Technique: Triple accordion fold

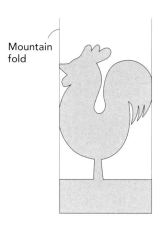

Mountain fold

15 Grazing Grass *(Shown on page 10)*

Materials: One 6" (15 cm) square sheet of origami paper in green

Folding Technique: Quadruple accordion fold

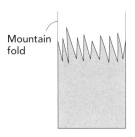

Mountain fold

17 Pigsty *(Shown on page 10)*

Materials: One 6" (15 cm) square sheet of origami paper in pink

Folding Technique: Double accordion fold

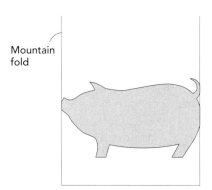

Mountain fold

16 Sheep Repeat *(Shown on page 10)*

Materials: One 6" (15 cm) square sheet of origami paper in white / Colored pencils

Folding Technique: Double accordion fold

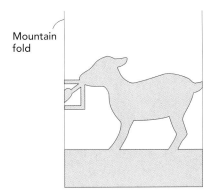

Mountain fold

Finishing Touches

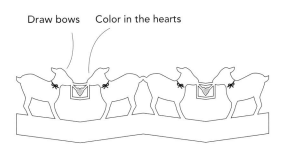

Draw bows   Color in the hearts

18 Sailboat Race *(Shown on page 11)*

Materials: One 6" (15 cm) square sheet of origami paper in red

Folding Technique: Triple accordion fold

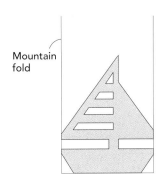

Mountain fold

19 Whale Watch *(Shown on page 11)*

Materials: One 6" (15 cm) square sheet of origami paper in navy blue

Folding Technique: Double accordion fold

Mountain fold

20 Wild Wave *(Shown on page 11)*

Materials: One 6" (15 cm) square sheet of origami paper in blue or light blue

Folding Technique: Quadruple accordion fold

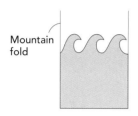

21 Penguin Family *(Shown on page 11)*

Materials: One 6" (15 cm) square sheet of origami paper in black

Folding Technique: Double accordion fold

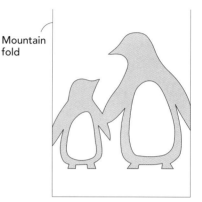

22 Anchors Aweigh *(Shown on page 11)*

Materials: One 6" (15 cm) square sheet of origami paper in blue

Folding Technique: Quadruple accordion fold

27 Balancing Act *(Shown on page 12)*

Materials: One 6" (15 cm) square sheet of origami paper in light pink

Folding Technique: Double accordion fold

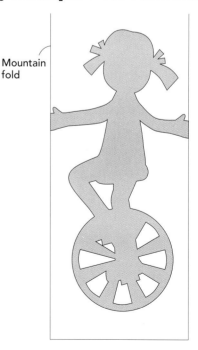

24 Rain Dance *(Shown on page 12)*

Materials: One 6" (15 cm) square sheet of origami
paper in blue

Folding Technique: Triple accordion fold

Mountain
fold

25 Love to Dance *(Shown on page 12)*

Materials: One 6" (15 cm) square sheet of origami
paper in mint green

Folding Technique: Triple accordion fold

Mountain
fold

23 School of Fish *(Shown on page 11)*

Materials: One 6" (15 cm) square sheet of origami paper in red or blue

Folding Technique: Triple accordion fold

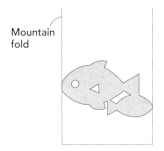

26 Fluffy Clouds *(Shown on page 12)*

Materials: One 6" (15 cm) square sheet of origami paper in blue

Folding Technique: Quadruple accordion fold

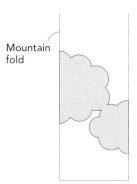

28 Carousel *(Shown on page 13)*

Materials: One 6" (15 cm) square sheet of origami paper in blue

Folding Technique: Double accordion fold

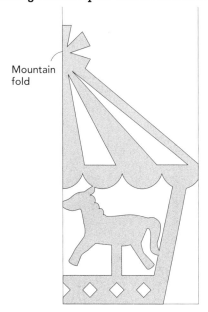

29 Circus Seals *(Shown on page 13)*

Materials: One 6" (15 cm) square sheet of origami paper in maroon

Folding Technique: Double accordion fold

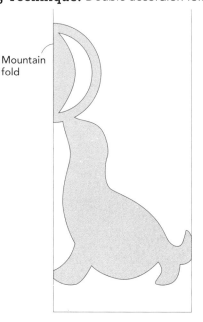

30 Camel Crew *(Shown on page 13)*

Materials: One 6" (15 cm) square sheet of origami paper in beige

Folding Technique: Double accordion fold

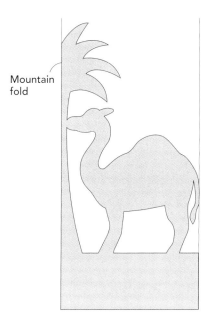

Mountain fold

31 Siamese Cats *(Shown on page 14)*

Materials: One 6" (15 cm) square sheet of origami paper in dark blue

Folding Technique: Quadruple accordion fold

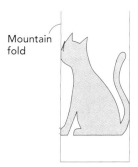

Mountain fold

32 Flower Baskets *(Shown on page 14)*

Materials: One 6" (15 cm) square sheet of origami paper in teal

Folding Technique: Triple accordion fold

Mountain fold

33 Flower Vases *(Shown on page 14)*

Materials: One 6" (15 cm) square sheet of origami paper in brown

Folding Technique: Triple accordion fold

Mountain fold

34 Blooming Bouquets *(Shown on page 14)*

Materials: One 6" (15 cm) square sheet of origami paper in dark green

Folding Technique: Triple accordion fold

Mountain fold

35 Dangled Delights *(Shown on page 15)*

Materials: One 6" (15 cm) square sheet of origami paper in light pink or light blue / Thread

Folding Technique: Triple accordion fold

Use Blooming Bouquets template above.

Finishing Touches

③

② ①

Glue wrong sides of paper together following steps 1-3

Puncture holes in paper and insert thread through all layers

¹/₁₆" (0.2 cm)

Hang using thread

36 Paper Doll's Birdcage *(Shown on page 15)*

Materials: One 6" (15 cm) square sheet of origami paper in light green

Folding Technique: Triple accordion fold

Finishing Touches

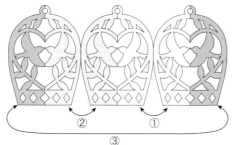

Glue wrong sides of paper together following steps 1-3

Insert thread through hole and tie to hang

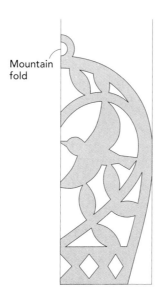

Mountain fold

37 Paper Perfume with Ribbon

(Shown on page 15)

Materials: One 6" (15 cm) square sheet of origami paper in light purple

Folding Technique: Quadruple accordion fold

Mountain fold

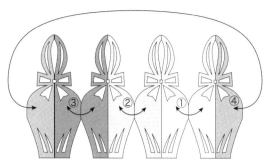

Glue wrong sides of paper together following steps 1-4

---

38 Paper Perfume with Flower

(Shown on page 15)

Materials: One 6" (15 cm) square sheet of origami paper in light pink

Folding Technique: Quadruple accordion fold

Mountain fold

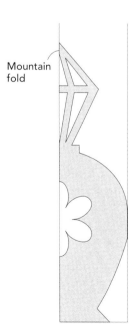

Refer to Project 37 above for Finishing Touches instructions

39 Frolicking Frogs *(Shown on page 16)*

Materials: One 6" (15 cm) square sheet of origami paper in light green

Folding Technique: Quadruple geometric fold

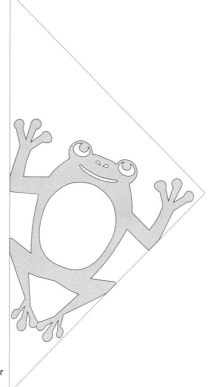

Mountain fold center

40 Party Parrots *(Shown on page 16)*

Materials: One 6" (15 cm) square sheet of origami paper in purple

Folding Technique: Quadruple geometric fold

Mountain fold center

41 Bouncing Bunnies *(Shown on page 17)*

Materials: One 6" (15 cm) square sheet of origami paper in pink

Folding Technique: Quadruple geometric fold

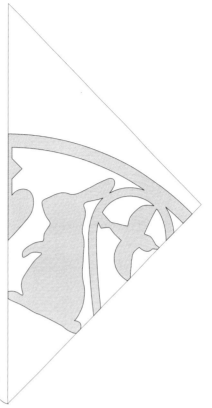

Mountain fold center

42 Nutty Squirrels *(Shown on page 17)*

Materials: One 6" (15 cm) square sheet of origami paper in maroon

Folding Technique: Quadruple geometric fold

Mountain fold center

43 Eight Point Flake

(Shown on page 18)

Materials: One 6" (15 cm) square sheet of origami paper in white

Folding Technique:
Quadruple geometric fold

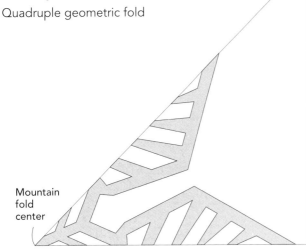

Mountain fold center

44 Quilted Flake

(Shown on page 18)

Materials: One 6" (15 cm) square sheet of origami paper in white

Folding Technique:
Quadruple geometric fold

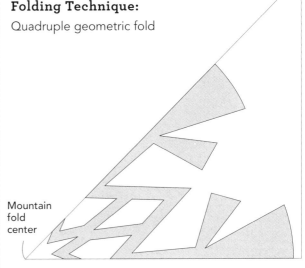

Mountain fold center

45 Lace Flake

(Shown on page 18)

Materials: One 6" (15 cm) square sheet of origami paper in white

Folding Technique:
Quadruple geometric fold

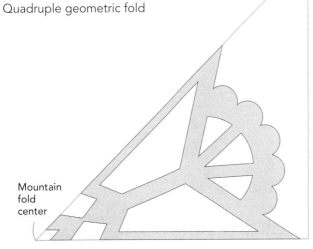

Mountain fold center

46 Carnival Flake

(Shown on page 18)

Materials: One 6" (15 cm) square sheet of origami paper in white

Folding Technique:
Quadruple geometric fold

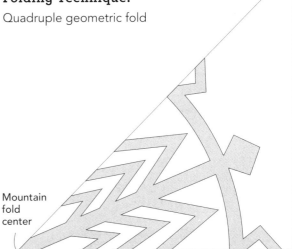

Mountain fold center

47 Star Flake *(Shown on page 19)*

Materials: One 6" (15 cm) square sheet of origami paper in light purple

Folding Technique: Triple geometric fold

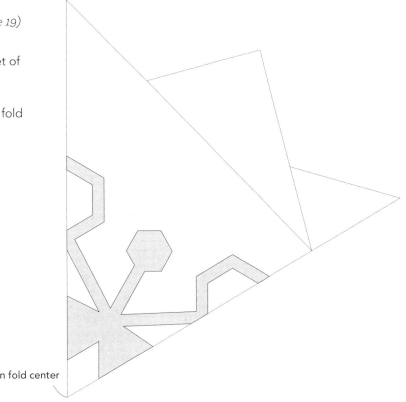

Mountain fold center

48 Poinsettia Flake

(Shown on page 19)

Materials: One 6" (15 cm) square sheet of origami paper in white

Folding Technique:
Quadruple geometric fold

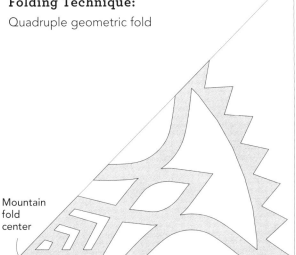

Mountain
fold
center

49 Firework Flake

(Shown on page 19)

Materials: One 6" (15 cm) square sheet of origami paper in white

Folding Technique:
Quadruple geometric fold

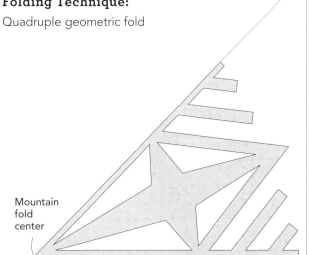

Mountain
fold
center

50 Diamond Flake

(Shown on page 19)

Materials: One 6" (15 cm) square sheet of origami paper in light purple

Folding Technique: Quadruple geometric fold

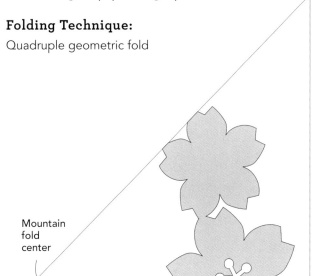

Mountain fold center

51 Gerbera Daisy

(Shown on page 20)

Materials: One 6" (15 cm) square sheet of origami paper in orange

Folding Technique: Quadruple geometric fold

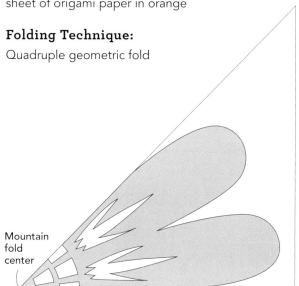

Mountain fold center

52 Cherry Blossom

(Shown on page 20)

Materials: One 6" (15 cm) square sheet of origami paper in light pink

Folding Technique: Quadruple geometric fold

Mountain fold center

53 Cherry Blossom Petals

(Shown on page 20)

Materials: One 3" (7.5 cm) square sheet of origami paper in each pink and light pink

Folding Technique: Single geometric fold

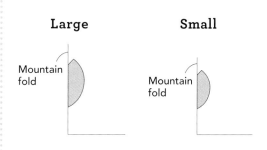

Large   Small

Mountain fold   Mountain fold

54 Dandelions *(Shown on page 20)*

Materials: One 6" (15 cm) square sheet of origami paper in yellow

Folding Technique: Triple accordion fold

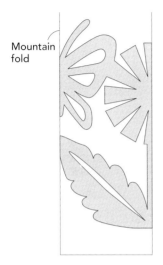

Mountain fold

60 Daylily *(Shown on page 23)*

Materials: One 6" (15 cm) square sheet of origami paper in orange

Folding Technique: Triple accordion fold

Mountain fold

55 Dianthus *(Shown on page 21)*

Materials: One 6" (15 cm) square sheet of origami paper in pink

Folding Technique: Quadruple geometric fold

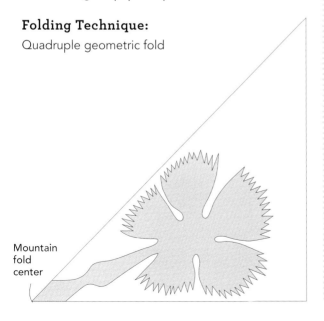

Mountain fold center

56 Anemone *(Shown on page 21)*

Materials: One 6" (15 cm) square sheet of origami paper in white

Folding Technique: Quadruple geometric fold

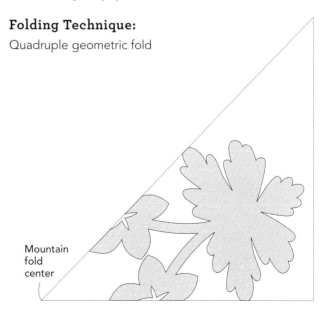

Mountain fold center

61 Large Hydrangea

(Shown on page 23)

Materials: One 6" (15 cm) square
sheet of origami paper in light purple

Folding Technique:
Quadruple geometric fold

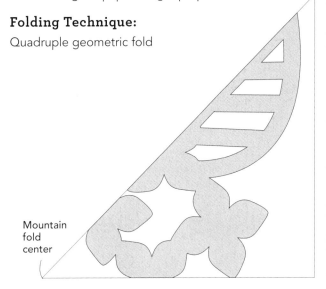

Mountain
fold
center

62 Small Hydrangea

(Shown on page 23)

Materials: One 6" (15 cm) square
sheet of origami paper in light pink

Folding Technique:
Quadruple geometric fold

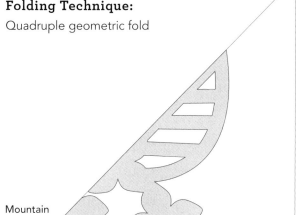

Mountain
fold
center

58 Sunflower

(Shown on page 22)

Materials: One 6" (15 cm) square
sheet of origami paper in yellow

Folding Technique:
Quadruple geometric fold

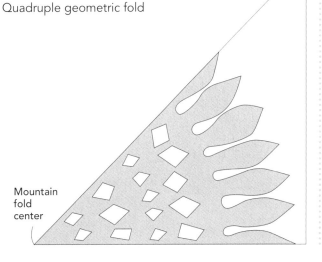

Mountain
fold
center

64 Ginkgo and Maple

(Shown on page 24)

Materials: One 6" (15 cm) square
sheet of origami paper in golden yellow

Folding Technique:
Quadruple geometric fold

Mountain
fold
center

63 Morning Glory

(Shown on page 23)

Materials: One 6"
(15 cm) square sheet of
origami paper in purple

Folding Technique:
Triple accordion fold

57 Lily of the Valley

(Shown on page 22)

Materials: One 6"
(15 cm) square sheet of
origami paper in light
green

Folding Technique:
Triple geometric fold

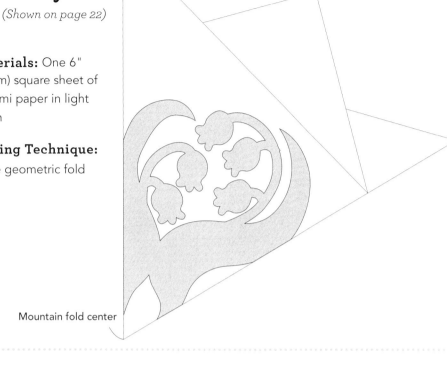

Mountain fold center

Mountain
fold

59 Roses

(Shown on page 22)

Materials: One 6"
(15 cm) square sheet of
origami paper in red

Folding Technique:
Triple geometric fold

Mountain fold center

65 Small Dragonfly

(Shown on page 24)

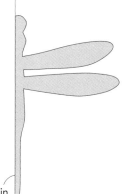

Materials: One 3" (7.5 cm) square sheet of origami paper in reddish brown

Folding Technique: Single geometric fold

Mountain fold

66 Large Dragonfly

(Shown on page 24)

Materials: One 3" (7.5 cm) square sheet of origami paper in brown or beige

Folding Technique: Single geometric fold

Mountain fold

67 Red Spider Lily

(Shown on page 24)

Materials: One 6" (15 cm) square sheet of origami paper in red

Folding Technique: Triple accordion fold

Mountain fold

68 Balloon Flower

(Shown on page 25)

Materials: One 6" (15 cm) square sheet of origami paper in purple

Folding Technique: Quadruple geometric fold

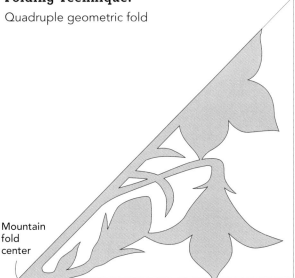

Mountain fold center

69 Japanese Aster

(Shown on page 25)

Materials: One 6" (15 cm) square sheet of origami paper in light purple

Folding Technique: Triple geometric fold

Mountain fold center

70-71 Large & Small Chrysanthemum *(Shown on page 25)*

Materials: One 3" (7.5 cm) square sheet of origami paper in yellow, dark yellow, or light yellow for each

Folding Technique: Quadruple geometric fold

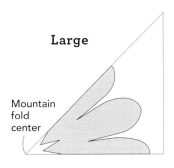

Large

Mountain fold center

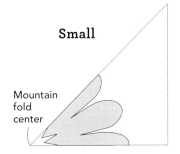

Small

Mountain fold center

72 Camellia *(Shown on page 26)*

Materials: One 6" (15 cm) square sheet of origami paper in red

Folding Technique: Quadruple geometric fold

Mountain fold center

73 Cyclamen

(Shown on page 26)

Materials: One 6" (15 cm) square sheet of origami paper in pink

Folding Technique:
Quadruple geometric fold

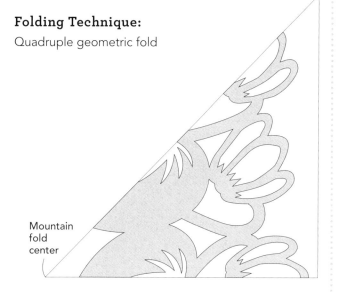

Mountain
fold
center

75 Large Snowflake

(Shown on page 27)

Materials: One 3" (7.5 cm) square sheet of origami paper in white

Folding Technique:
Quadruple geometric fold

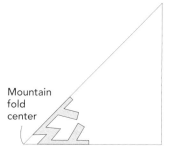

Mountain
fold
center

74 Japanese Plum

(Shown on page 26)

Materials: One 6" (15 cm) square sheet of origami paper in light pink

Folding Technique:
Quadruple geometric fold

Mountain
fold
center

76 Small Snowflake

(Shown on page 27)

Materials: One 3" (7.5 cm) square sheet of origami paper in white

Folding Technique:
Quadruple geometric fold

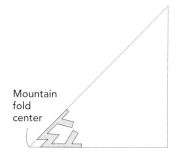

Mountain
fold
center

77 Small Star Snowflake

(Shown on page 27)

Materials: One 3" (7.5 cm) square
sheet of origami paper in white

Folding Technique:
Quadruple geometric fold

Mountain
fold
center

79 Large Star Snowflake

(Shown on page 27)

Materials: One 3" (7.5 cm) square
sheet of origami paper in white

Folding Technique:
Quadruple geometric fold

Mountain
fold
center

78 Christmas Rose

(Shown on page 27)

Materials: One 6" (15 cm) square
sheet of origami paper in beige

Folding Technique:
Quadruple geometric fold

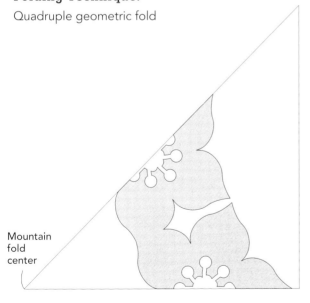

Mountain
fold
center

80 Sacred Bamboo

(Shown on page 27)

Materials: One 6" (15 cm) square
sheet of origami paper in red

Folding Technique:
Triple accordion fold

Mountain
fold

81 Clovers *(Shown on page 28)*

Materials: One 6" (15 cm) square sheet of origami paper in blue

Folding Technique:
Triple geometric fold

Mountain fold center

82 Daisies *(Shown on page 28)*

Materials: One 6" (15 cm) square sheet of origami paper in turquoise

Folding Technique:
Quadruple geometric fold

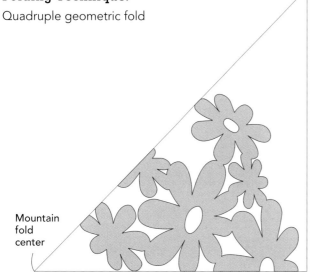

Mountain fold center

83 Zinnia *(Shown on page 28)*

Materials: One 6" (15 cm) square sheet of origami paper in purple

Folding Technique:
Quadruple geometric fold

Mountain fold center

84 Daffodil *(Shown on page 29)*

Materials: One 6" (15 cm) square sheet of origami paper in dark yellow

Folding Technique:
Quadruple geometric fold

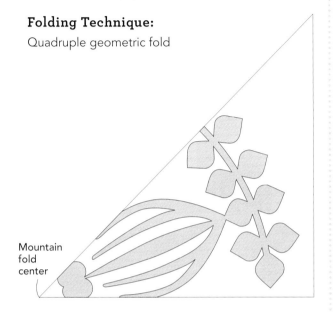

Mountain
fold
center

85 Large Roses *(Shown on page 29)*

Materials: One 6" (15 cm) square sheet of origami paper in red

Folding Technique:
Quadruple geometric fold

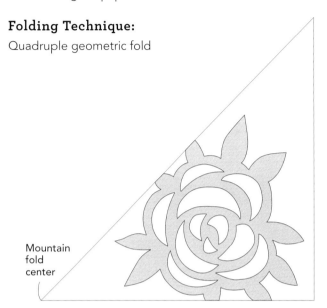

Mountain
fold
center

86 Carnation *(Shown on page 29)*

Materials: One 6" (15 cm) square sheet of origami paper in hot pink

Folding Technique:
Quadruple geometric fold

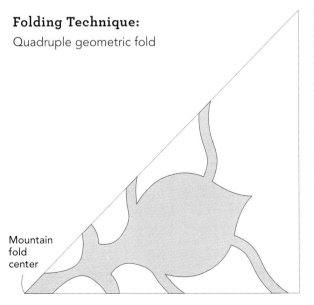

Mountain
fold
center

87 Four Point Leaf *(Shown on page 30)*

Materials: One 6" (15 cm) square sheet of origami paper in light green

Folding Technique:
Quadruple geometric fold

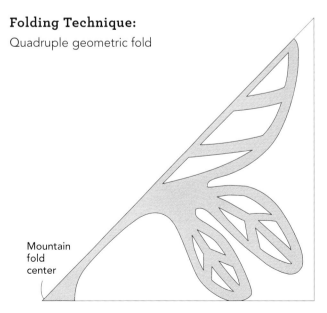

Mountain
fold
center

88 Six Point Leaf

(Shown on page 30)

Materials: One 6" (15 cm) square sheet of origami paper in green

Folding Technique:

Triple geometric fold

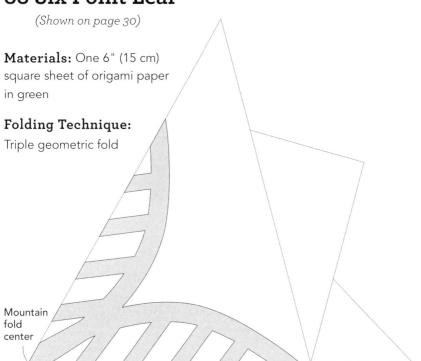

Mountain fold center

89 Leaf Trim

(Shown on page 30)

Materials: One 6" (15 cm) square sheet of origami paper in light green, teal, or turquoise

Folding Technique:

Quadruple accordion fold

Mountain fold

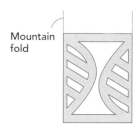

90 Flowering Leaf

(Shown on page 31)

Materials: One 6" (15 cm) square sheet of origami paper in mint green

Folding Technique:

Quadruple geometric fold

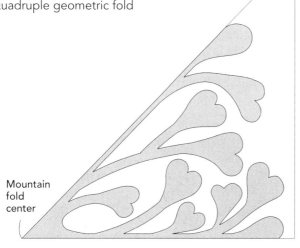

Mountain fold center

91 Leaf Wreath

(Shown on page 31)

Materials: One 6" (15 cm) square sheet of origami paper in moss green

Folding Technique:

Quadruple geometric fold

Mountain fold center

93 Field of Leaves

(Shown on page 32)

Materials: One 6" (15 cm) square
sheet of origami paper in light green

Folding Technique:

Quadruple geometric fold

Mountain
fold
center

94 Fern

(Shown on page 32)

Materials: One 6" (15 cm) square
sheet of origami paper in turquoise

Folding Technique:

Quadruple geometric fold

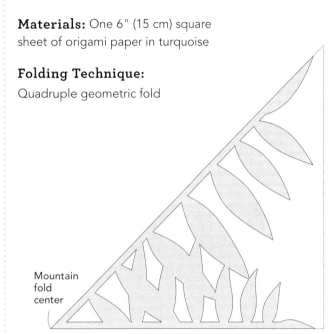

Mountain
fold
center

95 Scroll Doily

(Shown on page 33)

Materials: One 6" (15 cm) square
sheet of origami paper in white

Folding Technique:
Quadruple geometric fold

Mountain
fold
center

96 Garden Doily

(Shown on page 33)

Materials: One 6" (15 cm) square
sheet of origami paper in white

Folding Technique:
Quadruple geometric fold

Mountain
fold
center

97 Scalloped Doily

(Shown on page 33)

Materials: One 6" (15 cm) square
sheet of origami paper in white

Folding Technique:

Quadruple geometric fold

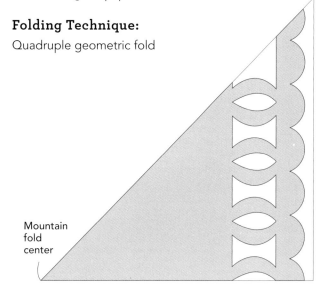

Mountain
fold
center

98 Star Spangled

(Shown on page 34)

Materials: One 6" (15 cm) square
sheet of origami paper in light yellow

Folding Technique:

Quadruple geometric fold

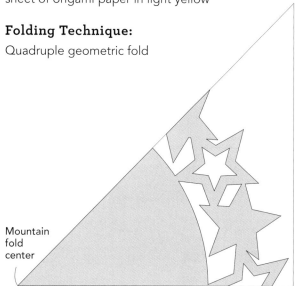

Mountain
fold
center

99 Hearts and Bows

(Shown on page 34)

Materials: One 6" (15 cm) square
sheet of origami paper in light pink

Folding Technique:

Quadruple geometric fold

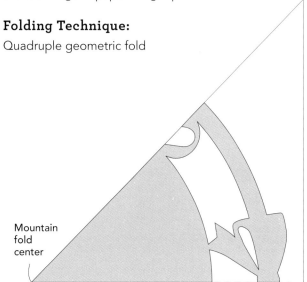

Mountain
fold
center

100 In the Garden

(Shown on page 34)

Materials: One 6" (15 cm) square
sheet of origami paper in mint green

Folding Technique:

Quadruple geometric fold

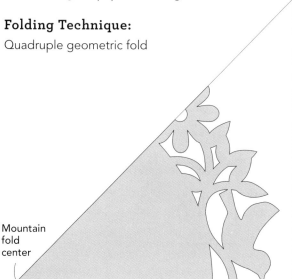

Mountain
fold
center

101 Flower Power

(Shown on page 34)

Materials: One 6" (15 cm) square sheet of origami paper in pink

Folding Technique:
Quadruple geometric fold

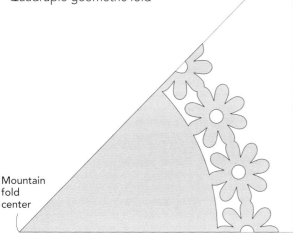

Mountain fold center

102 Ribbon Lace

(Shown on page 35)

Materials: One 6" (15 cm) square sheet of origami paper in white

Folding Technique:
Quadruple accordion fold

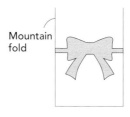

Mountain fold

103 Flower Lace

(Shown on page 35)

Materials: One 6" (15 cm) square sheet of origami paper in white

Folding Technique:
Quadruple accordion fold

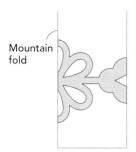

Mountain fold

104 Stitched Lace

(Shown on page 35)

Materials: One 6" (15 cm) square sheet of origami paper in white

Folding Technique:
Quadruple accordion fold

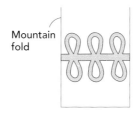

Mountain fold

105 Bow Lace

(Shown on page 35)

Materials: One 6" (15 cm) square sheet of origami paper in light purple

Folding Technique:
Quadruple accordion fold

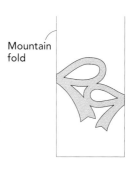

Mountain fold

106 Shamrock Lace

(Shown on page 35)

Materials: One 6" (15 cm) square sheet of origami paper in mint green

Folding Technique: Quadruple accordion fold

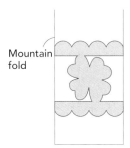

Mountain fold

107 Heart Lace

(Shown on page 35)

Materials: One 6" (15 cm) square sheet of origami paper in light pink

Folding Technique: Quadruple accordion fold

Mountain fold

132 Heart Cup

(Shown on page 40)

Materials: One 6" (15 cm) square sheet of origami paper in light purple or light pink / Cup

Folding Technique: Quadruple accordion fold

Use Heart Lace template at left.

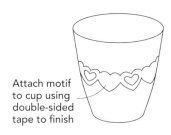

Attach motif to cup using double-sided tape to finish

108 King's Crown

(Shown on page 36)

Materials: One 3½" x 9" (9 x 22.5 cm) envelope in beige

Folding Technique: Double accordion envelope fold

109 Queen's Crown

(Shown on page 36)

Materials: One 3½" x 9" (9 x 22.5 cm) envelope in light blue

Folding Technique: Double accordion envelope fold

110 Flower Wreath

(Shown on page 36)

Materials: One 3½" x 8" (9 x 20.5 cm) envelope in mint green

Folding Technique: Triple accordion envelope fold

111 Lovebirds

(Shown on page 36)

Materials: One 3½" x 9" (9 x 22.5 cm) envelope in beige

Folding Technique: Triple accordion envelope fold

112 Village

(Shown on page 36)

Materials: One 3½" x 8" (9 x 20.5 cm) envelope in light blue

Folding Technique: Single geometric envelope fold

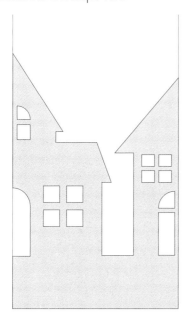

113 Matrioshkas

(Shown on page 36)

Materials: One 3½" x 9" (9 x 22.5 cm) envelope in beige

Folding Technique: Triple accordion envelope fold

114 Japanese Toy Mobile *(Shown on page 37)*

Materials: One 3¼" x 4" (8 x 10 cm) sheet of construction
paper in each red, yellow, and blue / Thread

Folding Technique: Single geometric fold

Finishing Touches

Leave top
thread long
for hanging

Tie knots

Temari ball

1¼" (3 cm)

Temari Ball (red)

Mountain
fold

Fan

Fan

Fan

Spinning top

Spinning top

1¼" (3 cm)   Tie knots

Spinning top

Puncture holes
in spinning top
and fan and insert
thread through
holes

Adjust thread to
1¼" (3 cm), knot,
and trim excess

Follow same
process to attach
temari ball

Fan (yellow)

Mountain
fold

Spinning Top (blue)

Mountain
fold

115 Japanese Botanical Mobile *(Shown on page 37)*

Materials: One 2¾" x 3¼" (7 x 8 cm) sheet of construction paper in each moss green, light green, and light pink / Thread

Folding Technique: Single geometric fold

Pine Trees (moss green)

Finishing Touches

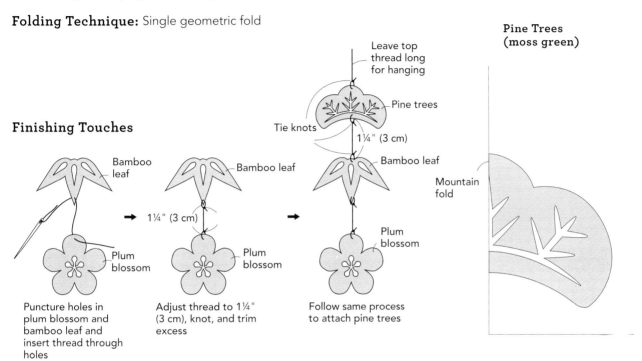

Leave top thread long for hanging

Pine trees

Tie knots

1¼" (3 cm)

Bamboo leaf

Plum blossom

Bamboo leaf

Bamboo leaf

1¼" (3 cm)

Plum blossom

Plum blossom

Puncture holes in plum blossom and bamboo leaf and insert thread through holes

Adjust thread to 1¼" (3 cm), knot, and trim excess

Follow same process to attach pine trees

Mountain fold

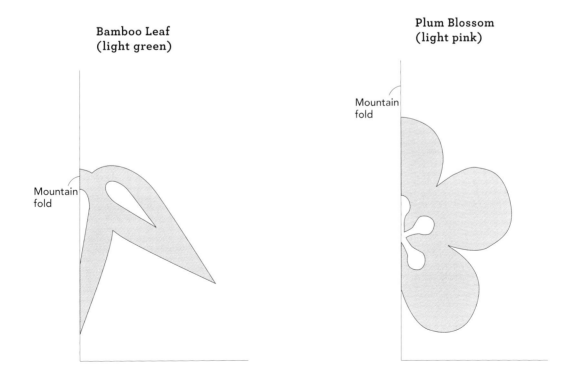

Bamboo Leaf (light green)

Mountain fold

Plum Blossom (light pink)

Mountain fold

116 Kagami-Mochi Money Holder *(Shown on page 37)*

Materials: One 3" (7.5 cm) square sheet of origami paper in red / One
2¾" x 3½" (7 x 9 cm) envelope in beige

Folding Technique: Single geometric fold

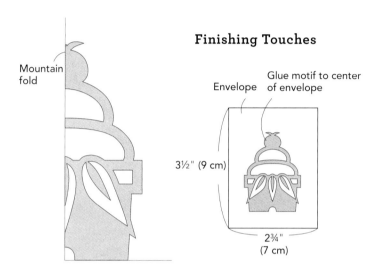

Mountain fold

Finishing Touches

Envelope

Glue motif to center of envelope

3½" (9 cm)

2¾" (7 cm)

117 Plum Blossom Money Holder *(Shown on page 37)*

Materials: One 3" (7.5 cm) square sheet of origami paper in each pink
and light pink / One 2 ¾" x 3 ½" (7 x 9 cm) envelope in light green

Folding Technique: Single geometric fold

Finishing Touches

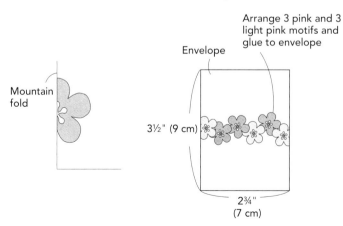

Mountain fold

Envelope

Arrange 3 pink and 3 light pink motifs and glue to envelope

3½" (9 cm)

2¾" (7 cm)

123 Bow Banner *(Shown on page 39)*

Materials: One 6" (15 cm) square sheet of origami paper in red

Folding Technique: Quadruple accordion fold

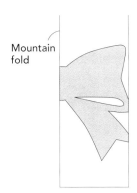

124 Cheers Chain *(Shown on page 39)*

Materials: One 6" (15 cm) square sheet of origami paper in magenta

Folding Technique: Quadruple accordion fold

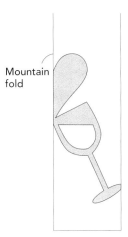

125 Four of Hearts *(Shown on page 39)*

Materials: One 6" (15 cm) square sheet of origami paper in red

Folding Technique: Quadruple accordion fold

118 Heartstrings *(Shown on page 38)*

Materials: One 2" x 11¾" (5 x 29.7 cm) sheet of copy paper in red

Folding Technique: Quadruple accordion fold

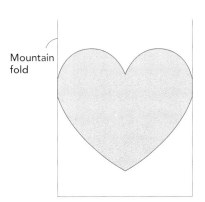

119-121 Fluttering Butterflies *(Shown on page 38)*

Materials: Paper A: One 2½" x 2¾" (6 x 7 cm) sheet of construction paper in purple, pink, or teal / **Paper B:** One 2½" x 2¾" (6 x 7 cm) sheet of construction paper in white

Folding Technique: Single geometric fold

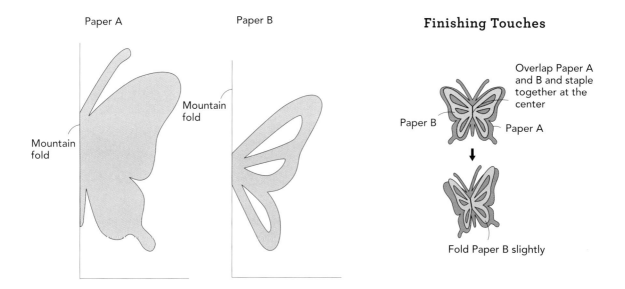

Paper A

Paper B

Mountain fold

Mountain fold

Mountain fold

Finishing Touches

Overlap Paper A and B and staple together at the center

Paper B

Paper A

Fold Paper B slightly

129-130 Butterfly Bags *(Shown on page 39)*

Materials: Paper A: One 2½" x 2¾" (6 x 7 cm) sheet of construction paper in pink or teal / **Paper B:** One 2½" x 2¾" (6 x 7 cm) sheet of construction paper in white / **Paper C (for lace trim):** One 6" (15 cm) square sheet of origami paper in white / Paper bag

Folding Technique: Single geometric fold

Use Fluttering Butterflies templates above.

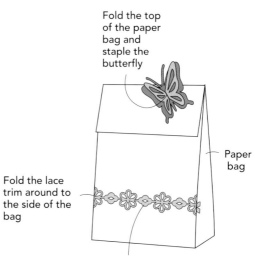

Finishing Touches

Fold the top of the paper bag and staple the butterfly

Paper bag

Fold the lace trim around to the side of the bag

For the trim, use the Flower Lace on page 95

122 Butterfly Swarm *(Shown on page 38)*

Materials: One 2" x 11¾" (5 x 29.7 cm) sheet of copy paper in pink

Folding Technique: Quadruple accordion fold

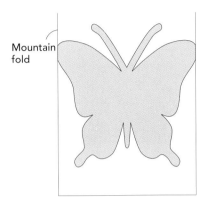

Mountain fold

126-128 Sweet Straws *(Shown on page 39)*

Materials: One 2½" x 4" (6 x 10 cm) sheet of construction paper in yellow, teal, or pink / Straws

Folding Technique: Single geometric fold

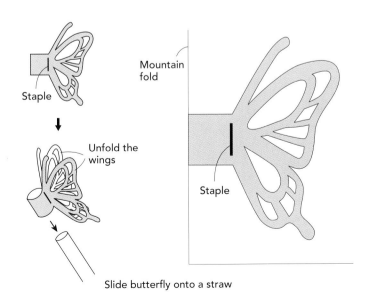

Staple

Unfold the wings

Slide butterfly onto a straw

Mountain fold

Staple

131 Cupcake Card *(Shown on page 40)*

Materials: One 3" (7.5 cm) square sheet of origami paper in pink / One 3¼" x 6½" (8.2 x 16 cm) sheet of construction paper in light pink / One 8¾" (22 cm) long ribbon in pink / Colored pencils

Folding Technique: Single geometric fold

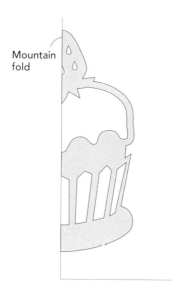

Mountain fold

Finishing Touches

Fold construction paper in half and tie with ribbon

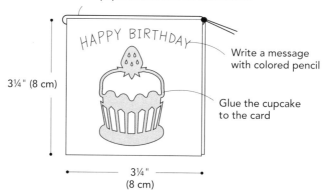

HAPPY BIRTHDAY

Write a message with colored pencil

Glue the cupcake to the card

3¼" (8 cm)

3¼" (8 cm)

133 Pumpkin Patch

(Shown on page 41)

Materials: One 2" x 11" (5 x 29.7 cm) sheet of copy paper in orange

Folding Technique: Quadruple accordion fold

Mountain fold

134 Bat Colony

(Shown on page 41)

Materials: One 2" x 11" (5 x 29.7 cm) sheet of copy paper in black

Folding Technique: Quadruple accordion fold

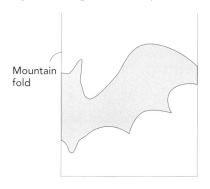

Mountain fold

135 Ghost Gathering *(Shown on page 41)*

Materials: One 2" x 11" (5 x 29.7 cm) sheet of copy paper in white

Folding Technique: Quadruple accordion fold

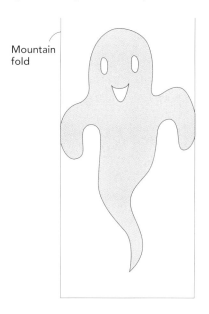

Mountain fold

136 Flapping Bat

(Shown on page 42)

Materials: One 3" (7.5 cm) square sheet of origami paper in black

Folding Technique: Single geometric fold

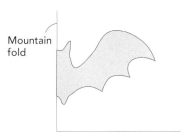

Mountain fold

137 Haunted House

(Shown on page 42)

Materials: One 6" (15 cm) square sheet of origami paper in black

Folding Technique: Single geometric fold

Mountain fold

138 Creepy Cats

(Shown on page 42)

Materials: One 6" (15 cm) square sheet of origami paper in gray

Folding Technique: Triple accordion fold

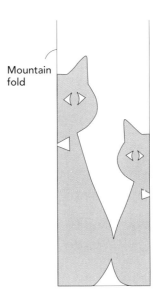

Mountain fold

139 Candy Chain

(Shown on page 42)

Materials: One 6" (15 cm) square sheet of origami paper in pink

Folding Technique: Triple accordion fold

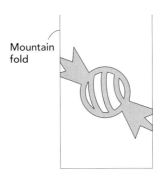

Mountain fold

140 Wicked Witches *(Shown on page 42)*

Materials: One 6" (15 cm) square sheet of origami paper in black /
One 4" x 4¾" (10 x 12 cm) sheet of construction paper in orange /
Colored pencils

Folding Technique: Single geometric fold

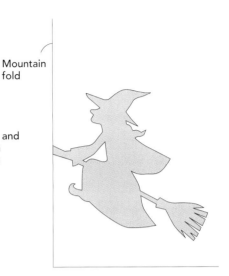

Mountain fold

Finishing Touches

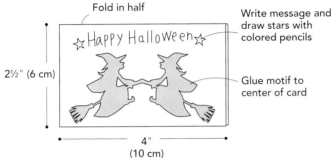

Fold in half

Write message and draw stars with colored pencils

Glue motif to center of card

2½" (6 cm)

4" (10 cm)

141 Spooky Lantern *(Shown on page 43)*

Materials: One 2¾" x 6" (7 x 15 cm) sheet of construction paper in black

Folding Technique: Double accordion fold

Mountain fold

142 Deck the Halls

(Shown on page 44)

Materials: One 6" (15 cm) square sheet of origami paper in light yellow

Folding Technique: Double accordion fold

Mountain fold

145 Plentiful Presents

(Shown on page 44)

Materials: One 6" (15 cm) square sheet of origami paper in pink

Folding Technique: Triple accordion fold

Mountain fold

143 Santa's Boots

(Shown on page 44)

Materials: One 6" (15 cm) square sheet of origami paper in orange

Folding Technique: Quadruple accordion fold

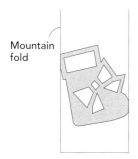

Mountain fold

144 Smitten Mittens

(Shown on page 44)

Materials: One 6" (15 cm) square sheet of origami paper in red

Folding Technique: Triple accordion fold

Mountain fold

146 We Can Build a Snowman *(Shown on page 45)*

Materials: One 6" (15 cm) square sheet of origami paper in white / One 4½" x 8" (11.5 x 20 cm) sheet of construction paper in dark brown / Colored pencils

Folding Technique: Single geometric fold

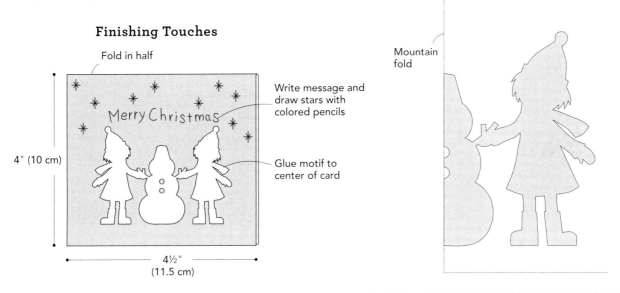

Finishing Touches

Fold in half

Write message and draw stars with colored pencils

Merry Christmas

Glue motif to center of card

4" (10 cm)

4½" (11.5 cm)

Mountain fold

147 Twinkling Trees *(Shown on page 45)*

Materials: One 3¼" x 6" (8 x 15 cm) sheet of construction paper in green

Folding Technique: Double accordion fold

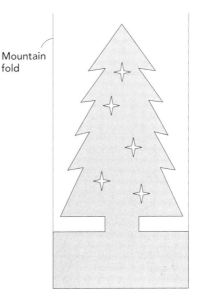

Mountain fold

148 Deer with Cheer *(Shown on page 45)*

Materials: One 3¼" x 4¾" (8 x 12 cm) sheet of construction paper in dark brown / 9½" (24 cm) of ribbon in white

Folding Technique: Single geometric fold

Finishing Touches

Divide ribbon in half and tie a bow around each reindeer's neck

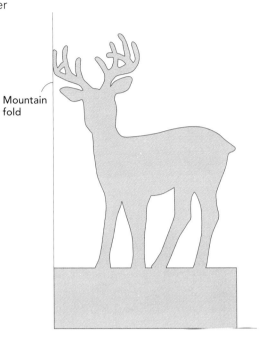

Mountain fold

149 Christmas Wreath *(Shown on page 46)*

Materials: One 6" (15 cm) square sheet of origami paper in dark green

Folding Technique: Quadruple geometric fold

Mountain fold center

150 Falling Snowflake Mobile *(Shown on page 46)*

Materials: One 7" (18 cm) square sheet of construction paper in white / Thread

Folding Technique: Double geometric fold

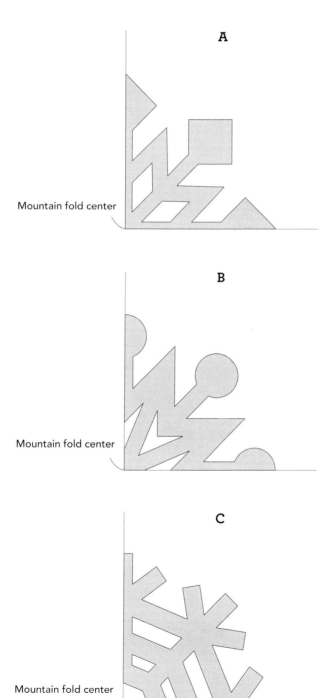

A

Mountain fold center

B

Mountain fold center

C

Mountain fold center

Finishing Touches

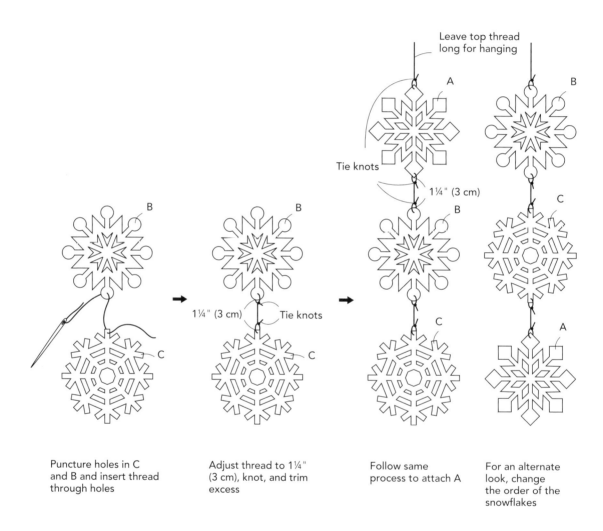

Puncture holes in C
and B and insert thread
through holes

Adjust thread to 1¼"
(3 cm), knot, and trim
excess

Follow same
process to attach A

For an alternate
look, change
the order of the
snowflakes